The Three Castles

Grosmont Castle
Skenfrith Castle
White Castle
Hen Gwrt Medieval Moated Site

Jeremy K. Knight BA, FSA

A History of the Three Castles

Three castles fayre, are in a goodly ground,
Grosmont is one, on hill it builded was;
Skenfreth the next, in valley is it found,
The soyle about, for pleasure there doth passe.
Whit Castle is, the third of worthie fame,
The countrey there, doth beare Whit Castles name,
A stately seate, a loftie princely place,
Whose beautie gives, the simple soyles some grace.

Thomas Churchyard (d. 1604), *The Worthines of Wales: A Poem* (1587).

'Three Castles Fayre'

The Monnow, a little river which flows into the Wye at Monmouth, forms the boundary of England and Wales, and of the modern counties of Monmouthshire and Herefordshire. The Welsh Marchland, from Monmouthshire up to Shropshire, is border country, distinct from other areas of Wales or England, to west or east, and with a personality very much its own. The Monnow valley forms a break in the natural defences of the southern Welsh border, an area of open pastoral country, though wooded and hilly, lying between the river cliffs of the Wye valley south of Monmouth and the Welsh hills around Abergavenny. Monmouth, the Roman *Blestium*, is on one of the major land routes into Wales, where a Roman road crosses the Wye, and forms a major gateway into south Wales from England. In this area, the Normans built a triangle of castles — Grosmont, Skenfrith and White Castle — guarding the routes of communication between Herefordshire and Wales.

Wooden Walls

A few months after the battle of Hastings (1066), William the Conqueror (1066–87) made one of his principal supporters, William fitz Osbern (d. 1071),

the lord of Breteuil in Eure, earl of Hereford. Fitz Osbern built castles at Chepstow and Monmouth, at each end of the river cliffs of the lower Wye, and from these bases the new earl overran areas of central and eastern Monmouthshire, including the later lordship of the Three Castles. There is certainly a trace of his presence — or that of his son — in the area, since the abbey of Lyre in Eure, of which fitz Osbern was the founder and patron, owned the church of Llangua, north-west of Grosmont, together with the tithes (one tenth of the produce) of the forest of Grosmont. Earl William did not enjoy the profits of his new lordship for long: he was killed in battle at Cassel in Flanders in 1071. Four years later, his son became involved in a rebellion against King William and forfeited his lands. Fitz Osbern's conquests — the later medieval Marcher lordships of Monmouth and Chepstow — passed to the Crown.

Opposite: Skenfrith Castle, together with White Castle and Grosmont, was one of a triangle of three castles established by the Normans to protect the routes of communication between Herefordshire and Wales.

The church of St James at Llangua (Monmouthshire), north-west of Grosmont, is the successor to a church that was owned by the Norman abbey of Lyre (Eure) from the late eleventh century. Llangua's connection to the distant Norman monastery is evidence of the activity of Lyre's founder, William fitz Osbern (d. 1071), or his son in the area of the Three Castles.

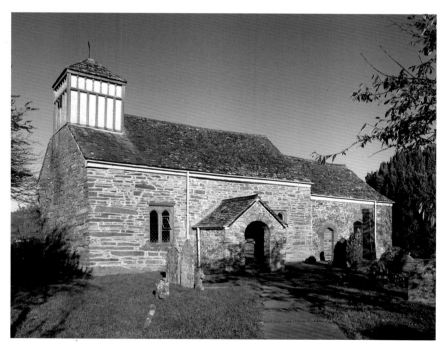

Below right: The Three Castles were first built as earth-and-timber strongholds. This scene from the Bayeux Tapestry shows the construction of an earthen motte, or castle mound, topped by timber defences (Musée de la Tapisserie, Bayeux, France. With special authorization of the City of Bayeux).

Below: The motte at Ewyas Harold (Herefordshire). Traditionally identified as one of a handful of castles raised by Norman favourites of King Edward the Confessor (1042–66), Domesday Book records that Ewyas Harold was refortified by William fitz Osbern, earl of Hereford. Fitz Osbern and other Norman lords used such earth-and-timber castles as instruments of conquest and domination as they pushed into Wales.

We cannot be certain whether the earliest castles at Grosmont, Skenfrith and White Castle were raised by Earl William, but if so, the defences — like all other local castles — would have been of earth and timber, and the internal buildings of wood and not stone. An early stone hall at Chepstow has previously been attributed to fitz Osbern, but is now thought to have been built by William the Conqueror: Earl William's castle was therefore probably of earth and timber. Nonetheless, it is clear that earthworks of early Norman castles do survive at both Grosmont and White Castle. At Skenfrith, evidence of their existence has been found by archaeological excavation, though they were levelled when the later stone castle was built.

These early castles would have served a wider role beyond the immediate military conquest of the Monmouthshire border country. They became seats of power and domination, controlling the land, its people (who were almost entirely Welsh), and its resources. The new Norman masters replaced the Welsh lords at whose courts rents and services had previously been paid.

After the rebellion of 1075, the Crown had no wish to see a single powerful magnate in possession of fitz Osbern's block of strategically important territory, and much of it was eventually granted away piecemeal: Monmouth to a Breton lord named Wihenoc, before 1086; Chepstow to the Clares about 1115; Llantilio Crossenny (the manor in which White Castle stands) and the rents of Grosmont to Payn fitz John, a royal official of Henry I (1100–35). When Henry I died in 1135, the Welsh rose against the Normans on the southern March and two or three years later King Stephen (1135–54) reunited the territory of the Three Castles in his own hands by exchange, to make a single unit for purposes of defence. In this way, the Three Castles came to be a single lordship, a block of territory that was to remain in single ownership until the early twentieth century.

The Medieval Lordships of South-East Wales

The first specific written reference to the Three Castles can be traced to 1162–63, when the sheriff of Hereford rendered accounts for expenditure amounting to £19 17s. 4d. on the garrisons and buildings at the sites. The picture becomes a little fuller towards the end of the twelfth century, at a time when the more important castles in the southern March were gradually seeing the addition of a stone hall or keep to their earlier defences, to serve as a central strongpoint.

Between 1177 and 1188 a royal official, Ralph of Grosmont, was supervising building work for the king at Hereford and at the Three Castles. We have no detailed building accounts, as we do with some later Welsh castles, but the total amount of money spent on each site is known. The detail is recorded in the Pipe Rolls, which list royal expenses. Indeed, Ralph was the first of a line of royal officials who have maintained the Three Castles, albeit with some interruptions, down to the present day.

In 1182 the Welsh attacked Abergavenny Castle, burning all save the keep, and killed the sheriff of Hereford at Dingestow, between Monmouth and Skenfrith, where he was building an earthwork castle. In the following year, Skenfrith and Grosmont were being prepared against possible Welsh attack and Ralph was provided with an official horse for his travel. The relatively small amount of money spent at Grosmont (just over £15 between 1183 and 1186), which was not enough for building in stone, suggests that the buildings there were still of timber, but between 1184 and 1186, £128 16s. was spent on the castle of Llantilio (White Castle). This probably paid for the stone curtain wall, which still surrounds the inner ward, and perhaps the small square tower whose foundations can be seen there. The £2 6s. 8d. spent on 'the dwelling in the tower of Llantilio' in 1186–87 sounds like the cost of fitting out and furnishing the completed tower.

In 1186 it was the turn of Skenfrith, where Ralph spent £43 17s. 7d., with further work in the following year repairing the palisades around the castle, and in 1190 there was work on the castle bailey. Excavation under the existing castle has found a large defensive ditch and a solidly built stone wall of twelfth-century construction. A Norman capital of red sandstone with scalloped decoration found on the site shows that a stone building of good quality existed here, and Ralph's work of 1186–87 probably included a stone keep or hall.

Above: King Henry I (1100–35, left) and King Stephen (1135–54, right), from the mid-thirteenth-century Historia Anglorum *by Matthew Paris. By Henry's reign, the Crown had granted away piecemeal the territory controlled by the Three Castles. Stephen, however, reunited the estates into a single unit in common ownership — principally for defence purposes (© British Library Board, Royal Ms. 14 C VII, f. 8v).*

Above left: Earthworks of the castle at Dingestow (Monmouthshire). The sheriff of Hereford was killed here during a Welsh attack in 1182.

Left: This Norman capital from Skenfrith Castle shows that a good-quality stone building existed there in the twelfth-century, perhaps a keep or hall constructed during building work in 1186–87 (Newport Museum and Art Gallery).

Hubtus de burgo dif
calciatus τ in camiſia
ſolū an altare de dyto
na: mortē orando grex
ta. Aduenuit eni cues
lond hoſtes cius

Hoc ... grertr ei duob; aluſ

Hubert de Burgh, 1201–39

In July 1201, King John (1199–1216) granted the lordship of the Three Castles to Hubert de Burgh (d. 1243). Hubert was a Norfolk man of modest family who had been a member of John's household since before he became king. By this time, the old twelfth-century castles with their square box-like keeps, plain curtain walls without flanking towers, and simple gate towers were becoming obsolete. New and more sophisticated types of military architecture were being developed by men such as Philip II ('Augustus'), king of France (1180–1223); by John's older brother, King Richard I ('Lionheart') of England (1189–99); and by the distinguished soldier of fortune, William Marshal the elder (d. 1219), whom King Richard had made lord of Chepstow (and much else) in 1189.

They built castles, which were often of geometrical plan — rectangles, trapezoids or polygons — with projecting circular towers equipped with batteries of arrowloops. Each face of the castle could now be swept by crossfire from longbows or crossbows. Keeps were no longer square, with corners vulnerable to siege engines or undermining, but round. At Chepstow, soon after he acquired it in 1189, William Marshal pioneered the use of the twin-towered gatehouse, with a heavily protected entrance passage between two circular towers. In short, what we think of as the typical medieval castle had been born. At one time it was thought that men like Richard I — who began to build Château Gaillard ('Saucy Castle') between Rouen and Paris in 1196, and strengthened the Tower of London — had brought these new ideas back from the Crusades. This now seems unlikely. All the necessary ingredients, including flanking circular wall towers and twin-towered gatehouses were already used by Roman military engineers in the late Roman city walls of Gaul, many of which still survive in cities like Le Mans or Carcassonne. These, and similar late Roman fort and town walls in Britain, may have served as models.

Hubert de Burgh's first priority may have been to provide himself with domestic accommodation in his new lordship. The rectangular hall block at Grosmont, with a hall and private chamber of suitable quality on its upper floor, may belong to these early years. By 1203 Hubert was away serving his king in western France. As constable of Chinon on the Loire, he defended the castle against Philip Augustus in a year-long siege until its

Left: The pioneering twin-towered gatehouse erected soon after 1189 at Chepstow Castle (Monmouthshire) by William Marshal (d. 1219).

Below: Hubert de Burgh issued this charter granting certain tithes from the forest of Grosmont to the Cistercian monastery at Abbey Dore (Herefordshire) around 1222 (Kenneth Spencer Research Library Ms. 191:3, University of Kansas, Lawrence).

fall in June 1205, after which he was a prisoner of war for two years. In the autumn after his capture, King John rewarded the loyal service of Hubert by granting his lordship of the Three Castles to his rival on the March, William de Braose (d. 1211), lord of Abergavenny. By 1207 William de Braose had also fallen from power, and he was hounded to ruin, and his family to their deaths, by a vindictive king. John's reign was not noted for his good relations with the barons of the realm.

By 1215, when the king was forced by his barons to grant the Great Charter (Magna Carta), Hubert had recovered much of his power, and had been appointed justiciar, the king's administrative deputy or first minister. It was not until January 1219, however, with the twelve-year old Henry III (1216–72) on the throne, that he recovered the Three Castles from the Braose heirs. Thereafter, Hubert is known to have visited the Three Castles at least three times between August 1220 and June 1222. He may well have been supervising the early stages of his new building work at Skenfrith and Grosmont at this time.

Opposite: Hubert de Burgh (d. 1243) is shown in this mid-thirteenth-century manuscript illustration taking sanctuary at Merton Priory (Surrey) during his fall from power in 1232. In the course of his eventful career, Hubert (earl of Kent 1227–32 and 1234–43) had two principal opportunities for building works at the Three Castles during his tenure of the lordship: 1201–04/05, and again between 1219 and 1232 (© British Library Board, Royal Ms. 14 C VII, f. 119).

Above: Dover Castle, where Hubert de Burgh led the heroic defence against the French in 1216–17 (© English Heritage Photo Library).

Below: Hubert de Burgh probably began to remodel Grosmont when he first held the lordship of the Three Castles between 1201 and 1204/05. This reconstruction drawing shows how the site may have looked in about 1203, when work had begun on building the rectangular hall block in stone, replacing part of the earlier wooden perimeter defences (Illustration by Chris Jones-Jenkins, 1991).

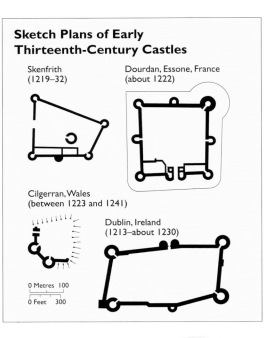

Sketch Plans of Early Thirteenth-Century Castles

Skenfrith
(1219–32)

Dourdan, Essone, France
(about 1222)

Cilgerran, Wales
(between 1223 and 1241)

Dublin, Ireland
(1213–about 1230)

0 Metres 100
0 Feet   300

The significance of these events for the understanding of the Three Castles lies both in their chronology and in the fact that Hubert — when he recovered them — brought to their rebuilding and modernization a wide and up-to-date experience of military architecture in England and France. He had added a hard fought defence of Dover against the French in 1216–17 to his earlier battle honours, had been responsible for many of the English king's castles in Aquitaine and had no doubt cast a professional military eye over the new castles being built by Philip Augustus in the Île de France around Paris whilst he was a prisoner. He now began a rebuilding programme on his Three Castles using this experience.

White Castle, which already had a stone curtain wall and square Norman keep, was not rebuilt in this phase. Its lack of high-status domestic accommodation, in contrast to Skenfrith and Grosmont, suggests that it was more a military garrison castle and there are

documentary references to supplies of arrows or crossbow bolts being stored there. Its two sister castles, on the other hand, were remodelled in accord with the most up-to-date ideas of military architecture and domestic comfort.

Skenfrith and Grosmont were rebuilt in masonry, using the durable red sandstone of Devonian age, which is so characteristic of buildings of all periods on the southern March. It could be used either as rubble masonry for wall building or for dressed ashlar for the sides of doors, windows or other openings. There was thus no need, as there was on many other castles, to use imported freestone, brought from a distance, for the finer work. Suitable stone could be quarried close at hand. A distinctive feature of both Skenfrith and Grosmont is that their towers are built over circular basements in which large quantities of supplies could have been stored. This was perhaps a reflection of Hubert de Burgh's experience of defending Chinon and Dover against prolonged siege.

At Grosmont, the earlier rectangular hall block was retained, but on the remaining sides of the Norman ringwork ditch, the timber defences were replaced with a stone curtain wall enclosing a polygonal area, backed against the hall block. Large circular towers protected three of the angles. At the fourth — between the hall and curtain — there was a gatehouse, which consisted of a rectangular block with a rounded front. The plan of Cilgerran Castle (Pembrokeshire), begun by William Marshal the younger (d. 1231) at Easter 1223 and perhaps completed by his brother Gilbert (d. 1241), is very similar. At Skenfrith, in a low-lying position on the floodplain of the Monnow, the ditch of the earlier castle was filled in and its stone hall or keep demolished. On the levelled site, Hubert de Burgh built an entirely new castle, sub-rectangular in plan, with a circular tower at each corner. Inside, he built a circular keep in the centre, rising above the surrounding curtain, and a hall and range of domestic apartments along its western side.

Above: An aerial view from the north of Cilgerran Castle (Pembrokeshire), which was begun by William Marshal the younger (d. 1231) in 1223 and is similar in plan to Grosmont (Skyscan Balloon Photography for Cadw).

Left: Hubert de Burgh is likely to have undertaken further work at Grosmont during his second tenure of the Three Castles between 1219 and 1232. This illustration shows how the castle may have appeared in about 1230, after the timber defences had been replaced with a stone curtain wall and towers (Illustration by Chris Jones-Jenkins, 1991; with modifications 2000).

The tomb effigy of King Henry III (1216–72) in Westminster Abbey. Hubert de Burgh exercised great influence during the early years of Henry's reign, but never fully regained his position after his fall from the king's favour in 1232 (© Dean and Chapter of Westminster).

Below right: The important border castle at Montgomery was begun in 1223 by Henry III in response to the activities of the Welsh prince, Llywelyn ab Iorwerth (Llywelyn 'the Great', d. 1240). In 1228, the king granted the castle to Hubert de Burgh.

Below: An army flees in disorder from a surprise attack in this mid-thirteenth-century manuscript illustration. In 1233, Richard Marshal (d. 1234), an ally of Hubert de Burgh, put Henry III's troops to flight with a surprise night attack on their camp outside Grosmont (© Photo SCALA, Florence, 2009 — Pierpont Morgan Library, New York, Ms. 638, f. 3v),

The years after Hubert de Burgh's recovery of his three castles in 1219 were prosperous ones for him. He was at the height of his power and influence with the young King Henry III. In 1227 the king gave him fifty oaks from the Forest of Trevil for the purpose of erecting his buildings at Grosmont. Then, in 1228, the king granted him the newly built royal castle of Montgomery, and the castles of Cardigan and Carmarthen in the following year. However, the failure of an expedition against the Welsh and the rivalry of the powerful bishop of Winchester, Peter de Roches (d. 1238), undermined his influential position. In September 1232, Hubert was turned out of office, deprived of his position as justiciar and stripped of his lands and castles.

Describing later troubles of Hubert, in 1239, the monk and chronicler Matthew Paris, who was well informed on the former justiciar's circle, singled out for mention his loss of Grosmont, Skenfrith and White Castle, along with Hatfield Peveril in Essex, which Hubert 'loved above all others, and on which he had spent an infinity of money'. Though he later recovered his castles, and to some extent the favour of Henry III, it is doubtful whether he was ever again sufficiently secure to risk arousing the suspicions of the king with further work on the defences of his castles. Skenfrith and Grosmont were thus probably substantially complete by the autumn of 1232.

On Hubert's fall, Richard Marshal (d. 1234), the son of his old ally William Marshal the elder, took his part against the king. Henry III assembled an army at Gloucester, marched against Richard's castle at Usk and besieged it. On 11 November 1233 Richard staged a surprise night attack on the king's army, which was encamped outside the walls of Grosmont. Caught asleep and unprepared, the royalists fled in disorder, leaving behind a large number of horses and much baggage. The king retired in haste to Gloucester. Hubert was reconciled to the king in May 1234, Peter de Roches having in turn fallen from power, but the Three Castles were initially withheld from him and placed in the custody of Walerund Teutonicus (Walerund the German), a royal servant who controlled a number of the castles of south Wales for the king. They were later restored to Hubert, but he was again in trouble with the king in 1239 over the marriage of his daughter, Megotta, and he was once more forced to surrender his castles. Hubert de Burgh, earl of Kent, died in May 1243.

The King's Castles, 1239–66

After Hubert de Burgh's fall, Walerund Teutonicus, back as constable, completed a room or chamber at Grosmont, which Hubert had left unfinished. The German constable also added a chapel there. At Skenfrith, in 1244, he was building another chapel and roofing the 'king's tower' (the round keep) with lead at a cost of £6 7s., as well as building a new hall, buttery and pantry at White Castle. Generally though, Hubert seems to have left his castles in good order, and we hear of no further work. In February 1254, they were granted to the Lord Edward, the king's eldest son, the future King Edward I (1272–1307).

The accounts of the steward of the Three Castles for the year 1256–57 have survived and give a picture of the rural economy on which the exploitation of the estates was based. There was revenue from market and mill, from pigs foraging in the woods, and from eels caught on a weir in the Monnow. Some Jews paid the lord 13s. 4d. for the privilege of living in Grosmont, but most of the entries refer to routine expenses on the estate and its buildings: the making of new wooden ploughs and the purchase of iron for their shares, new wheels for carts and wagons, or the thatching of farm buildings. There were reeves on outlying manors, carters and a smith, ploughmen, 'harrowers in winter', a man to keep the birds out of the corn in summer, and 300 harvesters.

At Grosmont, the bridge of the castle was being repaired, and ironwork bought for 'the new gate towards the field'. At White Castle, some money was being spent on a portcullis, an outer gate and a bridge, and it sounds as if new building works were in progress. There is no reference to costs of building in stone. The carpenters may have been fitting out buildings already finished, or the wages of the masons may have come under a different official. 'The tower' at White Castle — perhaps the old Norman tower — was having its roof repaired with lead and tin. A grimmer entry records payment for three pairs of manacles for the prison and bars of iron for the windows, followed by the brief note: 'For cutting off three heads, 3s.'.

In the following decade, the March was threatened by the rise of Llywelyn ap Gruffudd (Llywelyn 'the Last', d. 1282), prince of Gwynedd. In 1260 he took Builth, and a new constable, Gilbert Talbot, was sent to take command of the Three Castles. Two years later, Llywelyn annexed the lordship of Brecon and launched an attack on Abergavenny. The Welsh tenants of the border lordships rose in his support, and the constables of Monmouth and the Three Castles were ordered to garrison them 'by every man, and at whatever cost'. By the following spring Llywelyn's frontier lay only 4 to 5 miles (6.4 to 8km) from Abergavenny. Gilbert Talbot was ordered to prepare to defend the castles, but the attack on Abergavenny failed and the Welsh fell back. In 1267, however, the Treaty of Montgomery recognized the Welsh conquests and Llywelyn as prince of Wales. The Welsh were at their strongest and most powerful: such was the background to the refortification of White Castle.

With its Norman stone tower and curtain wall, it had once been the strongest of the Three Castles, but unlike its counterparts, White Castle had not been rebuilt by Hubert de Burgh and its defences

The Lord Edward, later King Edward I (1272–1307) — shown kneeling in this manuscript illustration — was granted the Three Castles in 1254, whilst heir to the throne (Bodleian Library, Ms. Douce 180, f. 1).

The accounts of the steward of the Three Castles survive for the period 1256–57 and provide a picture of the rural economy in the mid-thirteenth century. The lower part of this section shows the opening of the Grosmont (Grosmund) account (The National Archives: PRO, SC 6/1094/11).

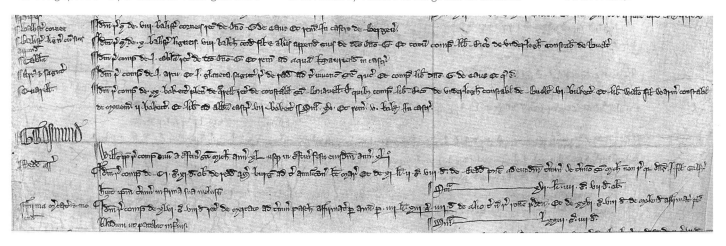

A late thirteenth-century decorated jug from White Castle (National Museum of Wales).

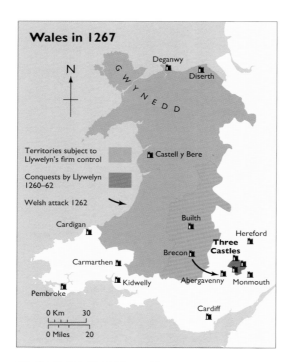

Wales in 1267

N

G W Y N E D D

Deganwy

Diserth

Territories subject to Llywelyn's firm control

Conquests by Llywelyn 1260–62

Welsh attack 1262

Castell y Bere

Cardigan

Builth

Hereford

Three Castles

Brecon

Carmarthen

Abergavenny   Monmouth

Kidwelly

Pembroke

Cardiff

0 Km   30

0 Miles   20

The tomb of Edmund 'Crouchback', earl of Lancaster (1267–96) in Westminster Abbey. In 1267, the Three Castles were granted to Edmund — the younger brother of the Lord Edward — and so began the long association of the lordship with the earldom and later duchy of Lancaster. Earl Edmund may have been responsible for some of the refortification work at White Castle (© Dean and Chapter of Westminster).

were now out of date. The reference to repairs to the roof suggests that the tower was still standing in 1257, but work on the new defences of the outer ward may have been well advanced by this date. It is frustrating that we have only the accounts for this one year.

Later, the tower was demolished as part of a rebuilding programme that transformed the defences. The original entrance to the castle had been next to the keep at the southern end of the inner ward, where a hornwork or crescent-shaped earthwork guarded the original line of approach. A new twin-towered gatehouse was now built at the northern end of the ward, and a series of four large towers added around the perimeter of the Norman curtain wall. Gatehouse and towers were equipped with batteries of distinctive cross-shaped arrowloops so that the castle could be protected by archers or crossbowmen firing across the water-filled moat. A postern gate and a further battery of loops were built over the demolished keep and gatehouse on the south. Beyond the gatehouse to the north, an earlier earthwork defence was enclosed within a stone curtain wall with four towers and a gatehouse.

The House of Lancaster, 1267–1399

In 1267 the Three Castles were granted to the Lord Edward's younger brother, Edmund 'Crouchback', earl of Lancaster (1267–96). This began a long association of the castles with the earldom and later duchy of Lancaster, which was to last until 1825. Edward became king in 1272. His subsequent conquest of independent Wales, beginning in 1277, and the death of Llywelyn ap Gruffudd in a skirmish near Builth in December 1282, rendered superfluous much of the military role of the Marcher castles.

Edmund of Lancaster died in 1296. Before March 1297 his second son, Henry (d. 1345), married Matilda, daughter of Sir Patrick de Chaworth (d. 1283). About 1310 their son, Henry of Grosmont (d. 1361), was born in the castle that gave him his name. About 1330 Henry the elder, who had been earl of Lancaster since 1327, became blind and retired to devote himself to religion. In 1333, he made over his castles and lands in Wales to his son.

Henry of Grosmont was a distinguished soldier, who fought in the earlier part of the Hundred Years War in France and was made duke of Lancaster in 1351. When he died ten years later, his lands were divided between his two daughters, Maude and Blanche. On Maude's death, Blanche, inherited the Three Castles and in 1364 her husband, John of Gaunt, was created duke of Lancaster. Their son, Henry of Bolingbroke, deposed Richard II in 1399 and became king as Henry IV (1399–1413). Grosmont, Skenfrith and White Castle were once again royal castles.

During the fourteenth century, the buildings around the inner ward at Grosmont were remodelled as apartments suitable for a noble household. The south-west tower was enlarged to provide a suite of well-appointed rooms on the upper floors, reached from the inner ward by a staircase set against the curtain wall. The north tower was largely demolished and replaced by two rectangular blocks housing suites of apartments. The tall octagonal chimney with a coronet-like top, which served its fireplaces, is still an impressive feature of the site. These additions, which turned Grosmont into a small, but very comfortable residence were either the work of Henry of Lancaster, before his blindness and retirement from the world in 1330, or that of his son between 1334 and 1361. Indeed, the castle appears to have been a favourite residence of Henry of Grosmont. It had a fine deer park that was

kept in good repair throughout the fourteenth century and would have provided him with hunting.

No significant additions were made to either of the other castles by the Lancasters, though the front of one of the gatehouse towers at White Castle was rebuilt at an uncertain date, perhaps after collapse.

Bare Ruined Towers

The Three Castles were now merely a minor component of the royal lands, rarely if ever visited by the king, their owner. They remained as local centres of administration, estate management and revenue collection. Repairs recorded in the royal accounts show that they were kept up, but they were no longer the homes of noble families, or border castles important for the defence of the realm. They saw a short return of their old military role in 1404–05 during the revolt of Owain Glyndŵr. In the summer of 1404 the Welsh were pressing hard on Abergavenny, but Richard Beauchamp, the young earl of Warwick (d. 1439), defeated them on Campston Hill near Grosmont. Shortly after this the Welsh routed the English at Craig y Dorth outside Monmouth, and pursued them to the gates of the town with great slaughter. On 11 March 1405 Gruffudd, son of Owain Glyndŵr, attacked Grosmont and probably besieged the castle, but a relief force sent from Hereford by Prince Henry, the future King Henry V (1413–22), defeated the Welsh; the prelude to an even greater Welsh disaster during an attack on Usk Castle on 5 May.

Left: Henry of Grosmont (d. 1361), born in Grosmont Castle about 1310, was created duke of Lancaster in 1351. A distinguished soldier, he served in France in the early years of the Hundred Years War. Grosmont appears to have been a favourite residence of Henry, who may have been responsible for the addition of comfortable new apartments. This illustration comes from the fifteenth-century Bruges Garter Book (© British Library Board, Stowe Ms. 594, f. 8).

Below left: The reverse of the great seal of Owain Glyndŵr from 1404–06 shows him as a mounted warrior bearing the royal arms of the princes of Gwynedd. The Three Castles last played a military role during the Glyndŵr revolt when his supporters threatened the strongholds of Monmouthshire in 1404–05 (National Museum of Wales, 92.74H/2).

Below: Prince Henry, later King Henry V (1413–22), sent a relief force to Grosmont in 1405 after it had been attacked and probably besieged by Gruffudd, the son of Owain Glyndŵr. Henry is shown standing on the left in this manuscript illustration of 1411–13 (© British Library Board, Arundel Ms. 38, f. 37).

By the late sixteenth century, when the map below was drawn, the Three Castles were essentially decayed and useless. Although Skenfrith appears to have still been roofed, Grosmont and White Castle are shown in ruins. Another fanciful drawing of White Castle (right) appears in a map of the area around Llantilio Crossenny produced in a case heard in the court of the duchy of Lancaster in 1571 (The National Archives: PRO, MPC 1/36 and 1/93).

This was the last time that the castles were to see active service. Under Henry VI (1422–61), repairs were carried out to the great tower, watergate and gate tower at Skenfrith, and new roofs and floors were put into the gatehouse and chapel tower at White Castle. But by 1538 the Three Castles were disused and abandoned, and the best that the antiquary, John Leland (d.1552), could say of them was that the greater part of their walls still stood. A survey of 1563 is even more explicit:

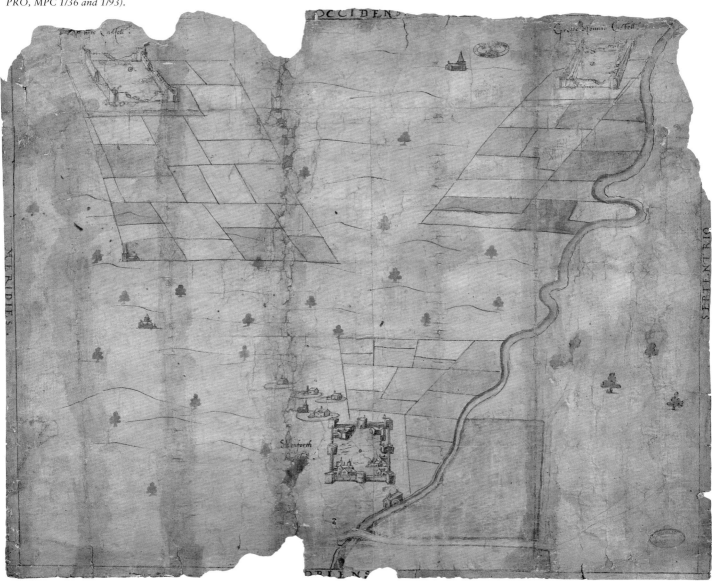

'The castle of Grosmont lackyth a bridge. It hath been a most fayre castle, and well and strongly buylded, butt nowe in ruyne and decay, sayving the utter (outer) walls thereof: and of late yeres part thereof hath byn covered, some with tyle. Tymber, iron and lead is rotten or taken away, and especially the barres of iron in the windows, and dores whereof late broken oute and taken away.'

The others were in no better state. By 1613 all three castles were 'ruynous and decayed tyme out of the memory of man'.

In 1825 the duchy of Lancaster sold the Three Castles to the duke of Beaufort. The Beaufort estate sold them off in 1902; it was the first time since 1138 that they had passed out of single ownership. White Castle was sold to Sir Henry Mather Jackson, a local landowner, and Grosmont (with the title of the lordship of the Three Castles) to Sir Joseph Bradney, whose *A History of Monmouthshire* is still a standard work. White Castle came into State care in 1922, and Grosmont in the following year. Skenfrith had several owners before being given to the National Trust. All three castles are now maintained by Cadw, the historic environment service of the Welsh Assembly Government.

Above: This late eighteenth-century watercolour of Skenfrith by John 'Warwick' Smith (1749–1831) shows the castle with the bridge and mill in the foreground (National Library of Wales, PD 702).

In 1902, the Beaufort estate sold off the Three Castles and for the first time since 1138 they passed out of single ownership. Grosmont, along with the title of the lordship of the Three Castles, was sold to Sir Joseph Bradney, the author of A History of Monmouthshire *(1904–33) (Gwent Record Office).*

A Tour of Grosmont Castle

The village of Grosmont (Y Grysmwnt in Welsh) lies below the castle, and a footpath from the village climbs gently up to its ruins. Large villages are not common in this part of the country, where the usual settlement pattern is a network of scattered farms. Size, however, can be misleading, and despite its present village appearance, Grosmont was a medieval borough. Until the 1850s, it had a mayor, a deputy mayor or 'ale taster', and a corporation. The large cruciform church with its spire is another result of the presence of the castle. Its dedication is to St Nicholas, who was little regarded in the west before his relics were stolen from Myra in southern Turkey in 1087 and brought to Italy. Thus, both castle and borough at Grosmont were probably Norman foundations, and not on the site of some earlier Welsh settlement.

At the top of the path from the village centre, visitors pass through a field gate to the flat elevated plateau on which the castle stands. Its walls and towers are straight ahead, but less obvious are the earthworks of an outer ward. These lie under the line of garden boundaries to the left of the gate, and then curve around from the gate to a point near the castle bridge. Close to the latter, where a steep scarp continues the line of the main defence, stone foundations of a rectangular medieval building of two rooms were found (probably a timber-framed storehouse or stable), which once stood in this outer ward.

The modern bridge across the castle ditch is on the line of its medieval predecessor. Indeed, the wooden support for the central trussel of the ancient bridge was discovered when the foundations of the present crossing were put in.

Within the inner ward itself the buildings are of three main periods: the earliest is the rectangular hall block, situated to your right, which originally coexisted with a timber defence around the rest of the castle's perimeter (see reconstruction, p. 8); in the second phase the timber defences were replaced by the stone curtain wall with three circular towers and gatehouse (see reconstruction, p. 9); and finally, in the fourteenth century, the towers and gatehouse were remodelled (see reconstruction, p. 23).

This tour suggests one route around the castle and describes the principal features of interest. It is not intended to be rigid and visitors may investigate the various parts of the castle in any order using the bird's-eye view (p. 25) or the ground plan (inside back cover). Our route, however, begins with the earliest stone building — the rectangular hall block.

Tarmac/gravel path from village centre. Rough grass path to wooden bridge across castle ditch. Uneven grassed surface inside the castle, with some stone steps. Stone steps to wall-walk via south-west tower.

Opposite: 'The castle of Grossemount ... standeth strongly on a rocke of hil drye ditched, and a village of the same name by it'. John Leland's description of Grosmont, recorded in his Itinerary...*, about 1538, remains an accurate depiction of the castle and village today (Royal Commission on the Ancient and Historical Monuments of Wales).*

Left: The seal of Hubert de Burgh, earl of Kent, who transformed Grosmont into a masonry castle in the early thirteenth century. The obverse (left) shows Hubert as a mounted knight, while the reverse (right) displays his arms (The National Archives: PRO, E 40/14374).

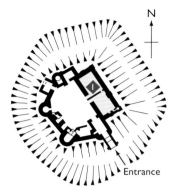

One of the early thirteenth-century chamfer stops in the doorway in the central cross-wall of the hall block.

Hubert de Burgh's hall block was probably the first stone building at Grosmont and replaced the earlier wooden eastern perimeter defences of the castle.

The Hall Block

The hall block was at the centre of life in the castle and provided comfortable public and private rooms for the household. Its architectural character shows that it belongs to the late twelfth, or to the early years of the thirteenth century. Although the curtain wall and towers were eventually built against it, the earth and timber defences were probably still standing when it was first erected. Since the amount of money spent on Grosmont before 1201, whilst it was a royal castle, does not seem large enough to account for such a building, the hall was probably raised by Hubert de Burgh soon after this date, and perhaps before King John seized his castles in 1205. The early documentation is, however, very scarce, and there are always pitfalls in arguing from negative evidence.

The hall block is built of coursed rubble masonry of local Old Red Sandstone, with shallow pilaster buttresses on its three outer sides and a sloping plinth at the base of the walls. The hall itself was on the upper floor, and initially it was probably entered from the courtyard by way of an external wooden stair (see reconstruction, opposite). This may have been done away with in later alterations, with the doorway converted into an additional window. The upper openings are, however, all much ruined and it is difficult to trace the original arrangements.

The ground floor is entered through a pair of door openings giving access to its two halves, on either side of a central dividing wall. The left-hand doorway still has the base of one jamb of a moulded surround of good quality. Both doorways were equipped with drawbar holes showing that the openings were part of the original structure of the hall block. Within, the ground floor of the block is lit by eleven tall, narrow lancet windows with stepped sills. A spiral stair to the upper floor is situated in the thickness of the eastern corner. It is set into the embrasure of one of the pair of windows at the 'lower' or service end of the block. There is a doorway at the far side of the central cross-wall and this has chamfer stops of an early thirteenth-century type. Its stones carry masons' marks — the 'signatures' of the individual masons who built it. One of these masons also worked on the dressed quoins of the outer corners of the block. The castle well is believed to have been on the lower side of the cross-wall. There is a fireplace in the centre of the southern wall, with part of its chimney surviving above.

On the first floor lay the hall itself. In considering the arrangements, however, it is important to bear in mind that medieval halls were very public rooms, accessible not only to the lord and his immediate followers, but to all the numerous members of his household. Consequently, it was normal to provide an adjacent room with more privacy — a solar or chamber — to which only the lord, his family and their body servants normally had access. Here at Grosmont, the spacing of the hall fireplace, together with its pair of flanking windows, suggests that there was a small square private room or solar for the

In this reconstruction of the original layout of Hubert de Burgh's hall block, the hall and solar (behind the wooden screen) are set above a pair of service rooms. Access between the two floors was by way of a spiral staircase at the lower end of the hall and by an external flight of wooden stairs from the courtyard, the position of which is conjectural (Illustration by Chris Jones-Jenkins, 1991).

household at the upper (northern) end of the block (see reconstruction, above).

The main hall, then, was a large rectangular room with a central fireplace in the north-east (outer) wall, whose broad, but shallow rounded recess can still be seen. The thin-bedded stones forming the walling of its back were carefully laid, the better to resist the effects of fire. The fireplace was flanked by a pair of large windows. There were two more windows at the lower end of the hall, and probably others in the now ruined wall towards the courtyard. The original doorway to the hall was also on the courtyard side.

During clearance and conservation in the 1920s, fragments of carved stonework were found in the rubble from this block, including pieces with carved 'stiff-leaf' foliage of early thirteenth-century date. This would seem to lend support to the attribution of the hall block as the work of Hubert de Burgh. Indeed, it is very similar to the hall at Christchurch Castle (Dorset), which Hubert had inherited through marriage in 1200.

Among the more exotic finds to have come from excavations at Grosmont Castle are these fragments of a fourteenth-century faience jar from Rakka in Syria — perhaps a relic of the Crusades (National Museum of Wales).

When first raised, the hall probably stood alongside timber defences crowning the remainder of the Grosmont earthwork (see reconstruction, p. 8). This timberwork, however, was soon to be replaced by the surviving curtain wall and towers, almost certainly in the period 1219–32. In fact, the details and general character of the masonry in both schemes are so similar, there can only have been a fairly short interval between the two. Some of the same workmen may very well have been employed on both occasions. The break in the work probably corresponds with Hubert's loss of his lands and castles between 1205 and 1219.

When Samuel and Nathaniel Buck visited Grosmont Castle, the gatehouse was still largely intact and its form is recorded in their print of 1732. The water-filled moat was a fancy of the engraver, who would not have seen the castle.

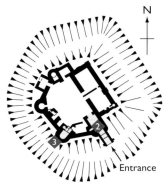

Projecting into the castle's deep ditch, the buttressed rectangular extension to the gatehouse was added in the fourteenth century to house a drawbridge pit.

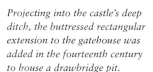

The doorway on the west side (left as you enter) of the gate-passage has a chamfer stop of an early fourteenth-century type, evidence of later alterations to the gatehouse.

The Gatehouse ◆2

You should now return to the gatehouse at the entrance to the inner ward. The masonry here is of two distinct periods. The inner part belongs to Hubert de Burgh's second phase of work at Grosmont and was built at the same time as the curtain wall and towers. Hubert had recovered possession of the Three Castles in January 1219. Construction was certainly underway by 1227, for in the March (the usual start of the building season) of that year the king granted him fifty oaks for erecting his buildings at Grosmont. The outer part of the gatehouse, however — together with its buttressed drawbridge pit — is a fourteenth-century extension. The Buck brothers' print of 1732 shows the gatehouse still largely intact, its front arch — which has now virtually disappeared — flanked by a rounded turret. As late as 1798, when it was drawn by Sir Richard Colt Hoare, the gatehouse and its front arch still stood.

It was originally a two-storey rectangular tower with rounded external angles, projecting forward from the curtain to give covering fire to its flanks. Only its south-western side now survives above foundation level. Here, three beam holes in the wall show the level of the timber ceiling of the gate-passage and of the floor of the guard chamber above it. At ground-floor level, two small doorways, one on each side, led from the gate-passage. That on the north-east (right as you enter) gave access to the narrow, flat berm between the hall block and the moat. The early thirteenth-century stops of its jambs (similar to those on the doorway in the cross-wall inside the hall block, or those in the other towers) show it to have been the work of Hubert de Burgh. At this point, the gatehouse can be seen to butt against the walling of the hall, in a way that shows it to be later work. On the courtyard-facing wall of the hall are traces of another stair, which must have led from the upper floor of the gatehouse out on to its roof. The doorway on the opposite side of the passage (left as you enter) has a later type of chamfer stop and belongs to the subsequent alterations. This door leads to the foundations of a stair that provided access to the upper floor.

In the fourteenth century, the gatehouse was extended to house a drawbridge pit in a rectangular buttressed projection. This also improved the archer's view along the outer faces of the curtain and on the western side of the extension. A single cross-shaped arrowloop survives, covering the ditch and curtain wall.

The South-West Tower

Originally the work of Hubert de Burgh, this tower was enlarged by the earls of Lancaster in the fourteenth century to provide a suite of well-appointed rooms on its upper floors. The imposing rear face of the rebuilt tower, with its tall entrance arch, faces on to the courtyard, but this has been added to the rear of the earlier round tower.

The three round towers built by Hubert de Burgh at Grosmont were all of a distinctive pattern, matched by those at Skenfrith, which he was building at much the same time. All had deep unlit circular basements suitable for storage. Here in the south-west tower the basement is particularly impressive. Above it you will see that the ground-floor chamber has three archer's loops set in splayed embrasures, with two-centred arched heads. The beam holes for its timber floor can be seen, and access to the basement below must have been through a trapdoor in this floor. The basement was probably filled in when the tower was remodelled.

In this remodelled form, the tower was entered from the courtyard by a low flight of steps leading to a landing under the entrance arch. Immediately

to the right, a spiral stair led to the upper floors, whilst to the left a straight joint in the masonry marks the junction between the thirteenth- and fourteenth-century work. Its lower part widens out into a slot, suggesting that a timber screen may once have divided off the ground floor of the tower.

The three floors above are all well appointed. The windows in their arched recesses on the upper floors look out over the church and village. Each of the two highest floors has a large fireplace in its north-west wall. That at the top still has chamfered jambs of pale cream ashlar, with a corbel above of Old Red Sandstone, which once supported a projecting lintel and hood.

The south-west tower was extensively remodelled for the earls of Lancaster in the fourteenth century. Two storeys were added to accommodate a well-appointed suite of rooms and the courtyard face of the tower was rebuilt to include a grand entrance arch.

The creasing in the stonework on the side of the south-west tower marks the upper end of a timber stair that gave access to the upper storeys of the tower from the courtyard. Above the creasing is the splay of a doorway that led to a first-floor gallery, perhaps timber built, that linked the apartments in the south-west tower with those in the north block.

The central courtyard at Grosmont, looking towards the north block created by the earls of Lancaster during their remodelling of the castle in the fourteenth century.

The upper floors of the tower could also be reached externally by way of a large timber stair set against the inner face of the curtain wall between the south-west and west towers. This was supported on two masonry piers. The jambs of the doorway into the stair passage can be seen in the further pier. Above the creasing, where the timber stair joined the south-west tower, is one splay of a doorway that led to a first-floor gallery, which must have been contained behind the wall-walk. This was perhaps timber built and linked the apartments in the south-west tower with those on the upper floors of the northern block.

The West Tower ◆4

This was again the work of Hubert de Burgh in origin. It is entered from the courtyard through a doorway, the stops of whose chamfered jambs match those of the same period elsewhere in the castle. The cylindrical basement has been filled in and lies under the present earth floor. There are archery loops, like those seen in the south-west tower, at three of the four floor levels; the second floor had no external openings. This tower was also heightened and considerably altered during the fourteenth century.

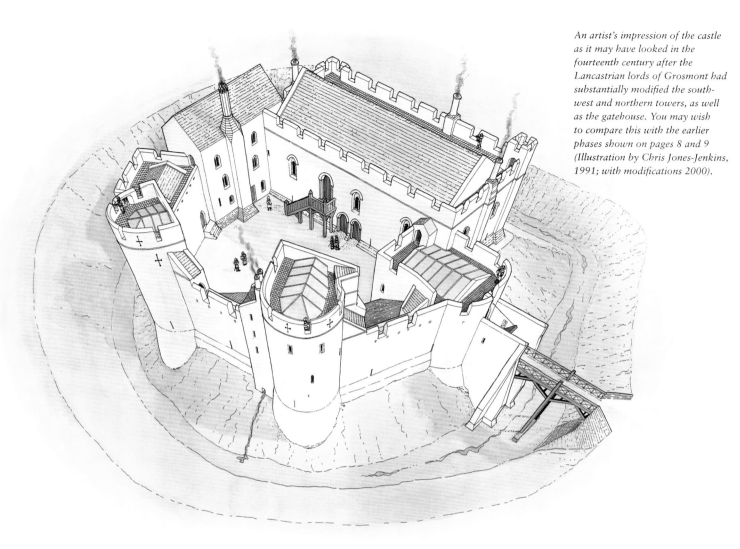

An artist's impression of the castle as it may have looked in the fourteenth century after the Lancastrian lords of Grosmont had substantially modified the south-west and northern towers, as well as the gatehouse. You may wish to compare this with the earlier phases shown on pages 8 and 9 (Illustration by Chris Jones-Jenkins, 1991; with modifications 2000).

The North Block ◆5◆

Dominated by its tall fourteenth-century octagonal chimney, the north block adjoins the western angle of the adjacent hall. From the plan (inside back cover), you will see that it consists of three separate parts, the centre one being the third of Hubert de Burgh's circular towers. This tower was demolished down to ground-floor level when the fourteenth-century block was built. The basement itself was filled in, but was cleared during conservation work in the 1920s.

Between Hubert de Burgh's round tower and the hall block to the east, there was originally a small postern gate, perhaps the 'new gate towards the field' mentioned in the accounts of 1256–57 (p. 11). This was also destroyed during the fourteenth-century alterations. The earls of Lancaster built a rectangular three-storey tower outside the line of the earlier curtain (see reconstruction, above). The scheme involved the blocking of the postern gate, with the two upper floors also extending over the area of the earlier round tower.

The ground floor of the new block was a single small room reached via a doorway from the courtyard. Next to this door, a window looks out on the courtyard and is fitted with a stone seat of moulded ashlar in its recess. The ground floor of the

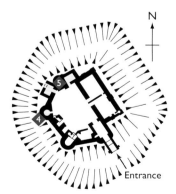

earlier round tower was reached by a stair from the room above, lit by two windows. The two upper chambers each occupied an entire floor. Both had fireplaces connected to the prominent octagonal chimney. Little remains of these, but in 1876 they were described as 'plain, but well wrought'. A door connects the first-floor chamber with the earlier hall block.

On the farther side of the basement of the round tower (and best seen from the exterior of the castle), the Lancasters raised another three-storey rectangular tower — the third component of the north block. This stood intact until the late nineteenth century. It is shown in the Buck print of 1732 (p. 20) and in a sketch of 1865, but its northern half had gone by 1904 and its internal arrangements are now difficult to make out. Built against the outer face of the earlier curtain, it was entered at first-floor level by a door through from the courtyard, possibly an altered window or arrowloop. The north-western half of this same floor level contained a deep window recess flanked by a latrine. Below was an unlit basement. The latrines emptied into the castle ditch through a tall arched opening seen in the Buck print. The upper floor of the tower would have had a second chamber, but a roof creasing inside the tower suggests that this may have become disused at a later period, with a new roof inserted below. Outside the curtain, a

sloping masonry glacis, contemporary with the fourteenth-century works, extends between the north block and the earlier west tower.

When considered together, the apartments in the north block, together with those in the remodelled south-west tower, would have provided suitable quarters for the earls of Lancaster. The high status of the rooms is emphasized by the tall octagonal chimney with its fine gabled and trefoil-headed openings at the top and a coronet-like cap. There can be no doubt that Grosmont was an extremely comfortable, if compact, country residence.

Back in the courtyard the visitor will see traces of various minor buildings, mostly lean-to structures, no doubt timber framed, built against the inner face of the curtain. One such building can be seen between the gatehouse and the south-west curtain. It must be late in the history of the castle for it is built against the stairs to the south-west tower, partly blocking them. The creasing for the roof of another late building can be seen in the outer wall face of Hubert de Burgh's hall block, between the present entrance and the gatehouse. The position of the door to this later building may be marked by an area of stone pitching. These late buildings would have served as lodgings for servants and lesser members of the household.

Above: The high status of the fourteenth-century apartments contained in the north block is emphasized by the tall octagonal chimney with its fine gabled and coronetted top.

The ruins of the north block viewed from the north-west, across the castle ditch. The base of Hubert de Burgh's north tower, which was demolished to ground-floor level to make way for the new buildings of the earls of Lancaster, can be seen in front of the chimney.

A Bird's-Eye View of Grosmont Castle

From the South-East

1 **Norman Castle Earthwork** — The great earthen mound on which the later stone castle stands; the 'gros mont' that gives its name to the site (p. 17).

2 **Outer Ward** — The flat plateau to the front of the castle gatehouse. There are traces of a medieval building in this area (p. 17).

3 **Hall Block** — Probably raised by Hubert de Burgh between 1201 and 1204/05. A first-floor hall and private chamber stood above a pair of service rooms (pp. 18–19).

4 **Gatehouse** — Built in two distinct phases, the inner part belongs to Hubert de Burgh's second phase of building. The outer part of the gate can be attributed to the remodelling of the castle by the earls of Lancaster in the fourteenth century (pp. 20–21).

5 **South-West Tower** — One of Hubert de Burgh's original three round towers, later extensively remodelled in the fourteenth century, and given a new arched entrance from the courtyard (pp. 21–22).

6 **West Tower** — Part of the early thirteenth-century work at Grosmont, this is the least altered of the three curtain wall towers (p. 22).

7 **North Block** Consisting of three separate parts, it was built over one of the thirteenth-century round towers. The block was built by the earls of Lancaster, perhaps while the castle was a favourite residence of Henry of Grosmont (pp. 23–24).

8 **Chimney** — One of the most prominent features at Grosmont. The striking fourteenth-century octagonal chimney served the fireplaces in the two upper chambers of the north block (p. 24).

(Illustration by John Banbury)

A Tour of Skenfrith Castle

'The castel of Skenefrythe', wrote John Leland in 1538, 'standeth five miles above Monmouth town, on the Mone river, on the very ripe [bank] of it, and in times past, by all likelihood, the river did goe around about the Castel dyke. Much of the utterward of the Castel yet standeth'.

Archaeological excavation at Skenfrith Castle (Ynysgynwraidd in Welsh) in the 1950s confirmed Leland's guess, and demonstrated that the outer walls of the castle were surrounded by a stone-revetted moat, like that still visible at White Castle, 9 feet (2.7m) deep and 46 feet (14m) wide, separated from the castle wall by a berm, 7 feet (2.1m) wide. On the east, the Monnow and the mill stream — from the adjacent corn mill — flow immediately outside the castle wall. To the north and west, the mown areas of grass outside the walls correspond fairly exactly with the extent of the ditch.

The walls of the castle form a sub-rectangle, with a tower at each corner. The western wall faces on to the main street of the village. The solid tower midway along its face was a later addition. Behind the outer walls can be seen the upper part of the round keep. Originally, this may have been topped by a substantial timber fighting top or hourd (see reconstructions, pp. 30, 33), with arrowloops through which fire could be directed against attackers on the outer wall or outside the wide ditch. In this way, Skenfrith prefigures — to some extent — the 'concentric' castles later built in north Wales by King Edward I.

The south-west tower, next to the corn mill, was refaced during restoration work in 1911–14, with an incorrect batter to its walling. Of the north-west tower, only the foundations now remain. From this corner, a short path beside the wall leads to the castle entrance.

From here, this tour suggests one route around the castle and describes the principal features of interest. It is not intended to be rigid and visitors may investigate the various parts of the castle in any order using the bird's-eye view (p. 35) or the ground plan (inside back cover).

The Vanished Castle

Except for the added tower on the outside, all the castle remains now visible were built by Hubert de Burgh in a short span of time, probably between 1219 and 1232 (pp. 7–9). Nevertheless, documentary references show that there had been a castle here since shortly after the Norman conquest; all was to be swept away for Hubert's new castle. The scale of the works associated with the new water-filled moat made it easier to level the old castle and begin again.

Archaeological excavations have shown something of the earlier history of the site. The castle sits on an artificial platform of gravel up to 12 feet (3.6m) thick, which is probably the spread mound of the early earth-and-timber castle. There is also much iron slag, the waste product of early iron making using bloomeries or small furnaces. Some of this slag may be Roman, for there is a scatter of Roman pottery from the site, but some may be early medieval. A large flat-bottomed ditch was dug along the slope between the river and the site of the later tower. This had traces of defensive timbering along its south-west edge. It was probably part of the defences of the early castle, but it has so far only been located by

Level grassed exterior. Wooden steps to the interior of the castle, with uneven grassed surface. Stone steps to hall and watergate.

Opposite: The castle of Skenfrith, which John Leland recorded in 1538, 'standeth … on the Mone river, on the very ripe [bank] of it'. The round keep dominates the castle and overlooks the surrounding curtain wall, and in this way prefigures the 'concentric' castles of the later thirteenth century.

Below: The castle was surrounded by a stone-revetted moat, the extent of which corresponded closely to the mown areas on the north and west sides of the castle.

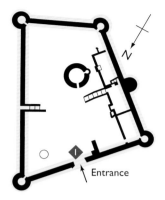

Medieval chess pieces from Skenfrith provide evidence of gentle pastimes at the castle (National Museum of Wales).

chance and beneath later structures in a small area north-east of the round keep.

The line of these early defences is still unknown, but geophysical survey has confirmed the evidence of excavation and found traces of a large L-shaped ditch between the northern and eastern sides of the central mound and the curtain walls. Early twelfth-century pottery from the lower fill of the ditch confirms its date, and a small iron furnace in its fill shows that smelting was still going on. It seems to have passed out of use fairly soon, for later a solidly built wall of twelfth-century masonry, obviously earlier than Hubert's existing castle, was cut through its fill. This may be part of the work for which Ralph of Grosmont was paid in 1186. Part of a scalloped twelfth-century capital of red sandstone (p. 5) suggests that a stone building of some quality, perhaps a hall or keep, was here at that date. Its proximity to the early ditch suggests that, like the early hall at Grosmont, it stood on the perimeter of the early defences.

The Curtain Wall and Towers

Returning to the visible standing remains, you will see that the entrance to the castle is now little more than a ruined gap. As at Grosmont, the drawing made by the Buck brothers in 1732 preserves for us the form of this entrance, a large and simple round-headed arch, raised somewhat above the then ground level, and no doubt reached across the broad moat by a bridge and drawbridge. Part of the arch had already fallen by the 1730s, and the remainder cannot have lasted long after this. Only the flat jamb

of this arch now survives, seen in the walling above and to the left of the entry. The Buck print shows a smaller round-headed arch above the main entrance, and part of a door leading to the upper floor of the gatehouse survives. Access from inside the castle would have been by way of a wooden stair. It is worth noting that neither Grosmont nor Skenfrith have the twin-towered gatehouses that we perhaps think of as typical of medieval castles. Though William Marshal pioneered their use at Chepstow soon after 1189, and the royal castle at Montgomery begun under Hubert's advice in 1223 has a fine example, twin-towered gatehouses must have been difficult and expensive to build at this date, and even important castles like Skenfrith and Usk were equipped with simpler forms of gatehouse

Before entering the castle it is as well to observe several other exterior details. The curtain wall, for example, is built of the distinctive Devonian Old Red Sandstone, so characteristic of Monmouthshire and the southern March. Its outer face (but not those of the towers) has a sloping batter, and the wall-walk along its top survives. The rectangular holes through the curtain, just below the level of the wall-walk, and at intervals of a little over 10 feet (3m), were probably for timber hourds or fighting galleries on the outsides of the walls (see reconstruction, p. 33).

Climbing the modern steps into the interior, on the eastern (left) curtain you will see the lower part of the outer parapet. Originally, this would have been about 6 feet (1.8m) high, to shield defenders, and was doubtless equipped with arrowloops at regular intervals. You will notice, too, on the two southern towers, the way in which the wall-walk

The entrance to the castle is now little more than a gap in the north curtain wall, but its form can be seen in this 1732 engraving, made from a drawing by Samuel and Nathaniel Buck.

was carried up steps, and around the parapet level of the towers.

The three surviving corner towers are all of closely similar pattern, with a deep circular basement — like those at Grosmont — and with two floors above, each with arrowloops covering the outsides of the adjacent curtain walls and the ground in front of the tower. The lack of fireplaces or latrines in the towers suggests that their function was purely military. Their entrances are well above ground level, at a height of about 6 to 8 feet (1.8 to 2.5m), and must have been reached by way of a wooden stair. There is no stair down to the basements, access to which must have been by a trapdoor and ladder from the room above. These dark basements, which then as now may have been prone to winter flooding, can only have been used for storage.

The north-east tower is typical. Here the ground level of the castle interior has been raised, and it is possible to look in with relative ease. On the first floor are three arrowloops set in arched recesses. The dressed stonework of the actual loops has gone, robbed for reuse elsewhere, and the openings are now larger than they were originally. The floor above had similar arrowloops. One, which has escaped robbing, has a long narrow vertical external slot with a triangular base (best seen from outside). There is the bottom of a similar loop in the added tower on the western side. The only other intact arrowloop, in the south-east tower behind the corn mill (and not easily visible from within the castle), is of a later cruciform pattern, and must be an addition. There is no surviving stair to the upper floor of the north-east tower, and it must have been reached from the wooden stair at the back.

Midway along the eastern curtain, a flight of steps leads down to an arched doorway through the wall, which served as a watergate.

The south-east tower is similar to that on the north-east corner, with a door raised well above ground level and a deep circular basement. A partly blocked opening to the left of the tower, with its threshold 5 feet (1.5m) above ground level, may have led to a latrine in the angle between tower and curtain wall. Once again, it can only have been reached by way of a wooden stair on the back of the tower. There is another arched opening to the right of the south-east tower. It is now blocked by the mill buildings, but may originally have been a sally port or postern.

The north-east tower — one of the four original corner towers that protected the angles of the castle. The one remaining intact arrowloop that survives from the period of Hubert de Burgh's work at the castle can be seen at the top of the tower.

The watergate in the middle of the eastern curtain wall gave access to the river Monnow, which flows just outside the castle wall.

Below: The entrance to the south-east corner tower (centre) is well above ground level and must have been reached by a wooden stair. The doorway to the left may originally have led to a latrine, while the arch to the right, now blocked, may have been a postern.

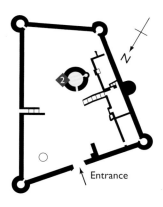

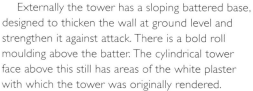

Opposite: The round keep stands at the centre of the castle. The earthen mound was heaped around the base of the tower after its construction. The cutaway reconstruction drawing below shows the keep as it may have appeared in the thirteenth century (Illustration by Chris Jones-Jenkins, 1991).

The south-west tower is of similar design to the others, and here the holes to support the floor joists are clearly visible. The tower in the middle of the west curtain is solid up to wall-walk level. The wall face of the curtain continues behind it, and it is an obvious addition, built against the original walling. The base of an arrowloop survives on the south.

The Round Keep ◆2

In the centre of the castle is the circular keep. The earth mound around its base is not, as was once thought, the remains of an earlier castle motte, but was heaped up around the tower when it was built, perhaps to give it greater protection from attackers. The keep was probably the last part of the castle to be raised. It has an internal diameter of 21 feet (6.4m) and has three floors: a basement and two upper storeys.

Externally the tower has a sloping battered base, designed to thicken the wall at ground level and strengthen it against attack. There is a bold roll moulding above the batter. The cylindrical tower face above this still has areas of the white plaster with which the tower was originally rendered.

The present ground-floor entrance is not original, but was cut through the walling at a later date. We know that the tower was repaired in 1448–49 (along with the gatehouse and watergate), but there must have been many unrecorded renovations during which the door could have been inserted. The original door is directly above at first-floor level. Beam holes can be seen on each side of its round-headed arch, and probably served as anchorage points for a porch over the external stair by which it was reached.

The ground-floor room was lit by two narrow loops, and the first-floor chamber had two large round-headed windows. The dressed stonework of the window surrounds, like that on the doorway, has mostly gone, no doubt robbed out for later farm buildings or the like. Originally, the windows may have been of two lights. There was no fireplace, and no stair down to the ground floor, access to which must have been by way of a trapdoor in the floor. Two corbels in the east wall would have supported the main joists carrying the floor above.

A very distinctive feature of the round keeps of the southern March is a semicircular projection, occasionally carrying a stair, or sometimes a latrine. Here at Skenfrith, one such turret carries a circular newel stair from the first floor up to the second and then on up to the roof. The upper chamber had two windows, a large hooded fireplace and a private latrine corbelled out over the face of the tower. Such a well-appointed room was clearly for a person of rank and was probably a *camera*, or — in modern terms — a sitting room and bedroom, for Hubert de Burgh and his family. The first-floor room would have been an antechamber to the more private apartment above. The accommodation in the tower probably corresponds therefore to that on the upper floor of the hall block at Grosmont.

In the thirteenth century, the tower would probably have been crowned by a circular timber fighting top or hourd, with arrowloops giving a very effective all-round field of fire. Slight traces of the beam holes for this wooden gallery survive at Skenfrith, and on a number of other Welsh round keeps.

Above: Philip II Augustus, king of France (1180–1223), built the round keep at Villeneuve-sur-Yonne (Yonne), in northern Burgundy, between 1204 and 1211. It is strikingly similar to Skenfrith (David Robinson).

Above centre: The round keep at Pembroke built by Hubert de Burgh's ally, William Marshal (d. 1219), probably soon after he recovered Pembroke from the king in 1200–01. It is perhaps the earliest of the round keeps in the southern March.

Above right: The round keep at Bronllys (Powys) was probably built by Walter de Clifford III (d. 1263), who took part in the Welsh war of 1231 with Hubert de Burgh.

The Round Keeps of the Southern March

The round keep had very definite advantages over the square box-like keeps usual in the twelfth century. It gave a much better all-round field of fire, had no 'dead ground' at the angles to give cover to attackers, and no corners which could be attacked with mine and ram. Though there are a few earlier examples, essentially the round keep was developed in the castle building of Philip II Augustus, king of France (1180–1223). His surviving keep of 1204–11 at Villeneuve-sur-Yonne in northern Burgundy, for example, is very similar to Skenfrith, with a first-floor entry above a battered base marked by an offset, and with a spiral stair to the upper floor.

Hubert de Burgh had, of course, fought against Philip Augustus in France. So, too, had his neighbour in the southern March, William Marshal the elder (d. 1219). Both men held (successively) influential positions during the minority of King Henry III (pp. 7, 10) and both had the resources to introduce new ideas in castle building picked up during their war years in France. Indeed, the full plan of Skenfrith is similar to King Philip's castle of the Louvre in Paris, on the site of the present museum.

The first circular keep in Wales was probably William Marshal's great tower at Pembroke, built sometime after he acquired his vast estates in south Wales and in Ireland by marriage in 1189, and probably later than 1200–01. It was at this time that he recovered Pembroke — the property of his wife — from King John (1199–1216), the area having been in the hands of the Crown since her father's day. Hubert de Burgh's position of true power and influence came some two decades after Marshal's initial rise to power. Both men, however, led the field in castle planning, and eventually several other round towers were raised by lesser lords who were military or political allies of William Marshal and Hubert de Burgh: men such as John of Monmouth or Walter de Clifford III (d. 1263) of Bronllys. But the round keeps of the southern March were not mere copies of French originals. They share a number of distinctive features not found abroad, including the roll mouldings at the top of the external batter, seen so well at Skenfrith, and the semicircular projecting turrets.

There are also a number of similar round keeps in Ireland, where the idea was carried by the Anglo-Norman lords who followed Richard de Clare ('Strongbow', d. 1176), his son-in-law William Marshal the elder, and Hubert's brother, William de Burgh ('William the Conqueror' of Connaught, d. 1205).

The Hall Range and Domestic Buildings ❸

Until the archaeological excavations of 1954, it was thought that none of the internal buildings of the castle survived, save for the round tower. However, the work revealed a range of buildings contemporary with the curtain wall and towers inside the western curtain.

The layout of this block of buildings can best be appreciated in plan view from courtyard level. Originally of two storeys, the ground floor had been filled in with gravel when the level of the castle's interior was raised in the late thirteenth or fourteenth century, in an attempt to combat winter flooding. The ground floor of the two northern rooms has now been cleared of its gravel fill, and is still prone to occasional flooding. These ground-floor rooms had probably always been intended as semi-basements,

though they are finished with good architectural details of early thirteenth-century character.

The range as a whole consists of three chambers, though the northern and central rooms were originally one, the present dividing wall being a later addition. At the northern end, later foundations, seen to the right, show that a further room once returned inside the north curtain, thereby forming an L-shaped block. Since this additional room faces east–west and adjoins the domestic buildings, it may have housed the castle chapel, which is known to have been built in 1244 (p. 11).

Today, the northern room is approached via steps and a ramped path that lead down past a small medieval window, which still has its medieval iron bars. The retaining wall on the right of the path is modern. At the bottom of the path there is a doorway of dressed ashlar stonework. All the openings in the towers and keep at Skenfrith would originally have had dressings of this quality, but elsewhere they have been robbed out for reuse. Masons' marks can be

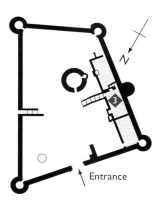

A reconstruction drawing suggesting how Skenfrith Castle may have looked in the mid-thirteenth century. The curtain walls and towers are all shown crowned with projecting wooden hourds, or fighting platforms (Illustration by Chris Jones-Jenkins, 1991).

seen on many of the dressed stones — the 'signatures' of individual masons, which also served as a form of quality control. Inside the east wall of the range are three vertical slots for wall post timbers supporting the roof. The upper part of these would have been blocked above the level of the new floor when the basement was filled in. The threshold of the doorway into this new higher level room survives on the wall top.

Returning to the grassed castle interior, what is now the central room is reached by a broad flight of stone steps. The doorway at their base still has its ashlar jambs with elegant carved stops on the outside, though the steps partially mask these, showing that they may be a later alteration. The room had two small windows, like that surviving intact in the northern room, and a blocked fireplace with crisply carved 'stiff-leaf' foliage on the capitals. It may have been blocked when it was found that periodic flooding made the range unsuitable for domestic use. Originally, this ground-floor range would have been the basement for a hall range at first-floor level. Our only real clue to the layout of the hall above is the position of the fireplace. The hall fireplace would have been directly above this, and served by the same flue. If, as was usual, the fireplace was located in the centre of the hall wall, flanked by a pair of windows, there would have been room for a square chamber, perhaps partitioned off in timber, at the northern end of the block.

The southern wall of the central room, beside the stair, has a recess in its centre which was originally a door.

There seems, however, to have been a change of plan whilst work was still in progress, and the initial doorway was blocked and a smaller door inserted beside it. This would have led either to the basement level of the southern room of this range, or to a stair leading to the upper floor at the lower (entry) end of the hall above.

At present, a stone stair leads up to the southern room, which is laid out at its higher level. In its east wall, it has the base of a fireplace, whose pyramidal stops (of a later type than those found throughout the remainder of the block) show it to have been an insertion, perhaps of the late thirteenth century. At the southern end of the range are the walls of a square tank (now filled in), which probably served as a water reservoir for the castle. On a site with the water table so high, there was no need for a well.

Across on the opposite side of the courtyard, the castle kitchens lay between the stairs to the watergate and the south-east tower. Two successive long, narrow buildings have been found in excavation (see plan on inside back cover), each with internal hearths for cooking and a large circular oven at one end, used for baking bread or meat. The lightly built foundation walls imply that both buildings were of timber. The kitchens are not laid out for display, but a large circular oven, found in excavation near the north-east tower, can be seen. Probably a bread oven, it may have stood within an earlier kitchen contemporary with the hall block. Part of another circular oven, with a rake pit for its ashes, can be seen built into the curtain wall by the kitchens.

A Bird's-Eye View of Skenfrith Castle

From the South-East

1 Site of Ditch — Marked by the areas of grass immediately outside the north and west walls of the castle (p. 27).

2 Site of Gatehouse — The original entrance to the stone castle is now little more than a ruined gap. Something of its medieval form is known from an engraving of 1732 (p. 28).

3 Curtain Wall — The outer face has a sloping batter at its base, and substantial sections of the wall-walk along the tops of the wall survive. A timber fighting gallery probably surmounted the curtain wall (pp. 28–29).

4 Corner Towers — All four were built to a closely similar pattern, with deep circular basements and two floors above. Equipped with batteries of arrowloops, their function appears to have been purely military (p. 29).

5 Watergate — A flight of steps leads down from the courtyard to an arched doorway, which must have served as a watergate (p. 29).

6 Later Tower — Added to the middle of the west wall, this tower is solid up to wall-walk level (p. 30).

7 Round Keep — At the centre of the castle, the keep contained a basement and two upper floors. The well-appointed room on the uppermost floor was intended for a person of rank and status. Such round keeps were a feature of the southern March in the thirteenth century (pp. 30, 32).

8 The Hall Range — A block of fine-quality chambers arranged inside the western curtain. The ground-floor rooms in this two-storey range were probably always intended as semi-basements. They were eventually filled in when the level of the castle interior was raised (pp. 33–34).

9 Site of Kitchen — Nothing survives above ground, but excavations have revealed successive phases of the castle kitchen in this area (p. 34).

During work in 2003 to protect the riverbank from erosion, the remains of a stone wharf were discovered just upstream from the castle. Associated artefacts indicate that it may have been in use during the building of the castle in the early thirteenth century. The wharf has now been reburied, but its position is marked by an information panel and paving slabs.

(Illustration by John Banbury)

A Tour of White Castle

White Castle stands on a low hill about a mile (1.6km) from the village of Llantilio Crossenny (Llandeilo Gresynni in Welsh). The Welsh form of the name, Castell Gwyn, is said to derive from a local ruler of early Norman times, Gwyn ap Gwaethfoed, but the original name of the castle was Llantilio Castle, and the alternative — first recorded in the thirteenth century — refers to the white rendering that is still visible on parts of the exterior walls.

The earthworks of White Castle comprise three separate enclosures (see plan on inside back cover). In the centre is the pear-shaped inner ward, surrounded by a wet moat with stone-revetted sides, containing the walls and towers of the main defences of the castle. To the south is a crescent-shaped hornwork. On the north — the side from which visitors approach the castle — is an outer ward with its own stone curtain wall, towers, and gatehouse surmounting the basic earthworks. Initially, this third area was part of a much larger outer enclosure that surrounded the entire eastern half of the castle. Some traces of its defensive bank can be seen on the ground, but it is much clearer when seen in an aerial photograph.

Originally, when the defences at White Castle were still of earth and timber, the site was entered from the south. The crescentic hornwork then covered the main approach to the castle. The outer ward, which may have formed a defended enclosure where armies in the field could camp without fear of surprise attack, was tucked into the rear. Indeed, episodes such as that on the night of 11 November 1233 (p.10), when a surprise attack routed King Henry III and his army camped outside the walls of Grosmont, were to be prevented if possible. Usk Castle has the same earthwork plan and may date from the same period, perhaps as early as the time of William fitz Osbern (pp.3–4). In the thirteenth century, when most of the present stone defences were built, the whole castle was turned through 180 degrees. A new gatehouse was built facing on to the

outer ward, which now became the approach to the castle, with the hornwork relegated to the rear.

This tour begins at the outer gate to the castle and suggests one route around the castle. However, it is not intended to be rigid and visitors may investigate the various parts of the castle in any order using the bird's-eye view (inside front cover) or the ground plan (inside back cover).

The Outer Ward

From the gate into the site, a path leads along the outside of the moat of the outer ward towards the outer gate. Curving around the edge of the field to the left, you will see the bank of the much larger outer enclosure, which at one time surrounded this side of the castle.

Seen as a whole, the outer ward is an irregular grassy area enclosed by a stone curtain wall with four projecting towers and a gatehouse. Unlike the inner

Level gravel path from parking area. Wooden bridge into outer ward with level grassed surface. Short stone ramp to wooden bridge and two steps to inner ward. Level grassed interior; stone steps to gatehouse tower and the hornwork.

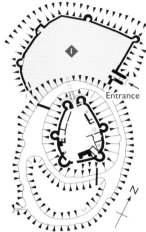

Opposite: White Castle's three enclosures run diagonally across this view. To the left (north-west) is the large outer ward, at the centre is the inner ward, with its high curtain walls and towers, while to the right (south-east) is the crescent-shaped hornwork, partially obscured by trees (Skyscan Balloon Photography for Cadw).

Left: Two of the projecting towers and the intervening curtain wall on the western side of the outer ward.

Above: The outer gatehouse at White Castle. Money was spent on its portcullis, doors and bridge in 1256–57.

ward and hornwork, however, its surrounding ditch is dry. Some traces of the earth bank, which preceded the stone curtain, can be seen on the western and northern sides.

In medieval times, the gatehouse into the outer ward would have been approached by a fixed bridge partway across the moat, with a drawbridge at its inner end. The pit for the drawbridge can be seen under the inner end of the present bridge. In each of the side walls, you will see a slot about 1 foot (0.3m) square, and these held the wooden beam in which were set the pivots on which the drawbridge and its counterpoise swung. Behind the drawbridge pit was a portcullis, the groove for which can be seen. In 1256–57, money was spent on making a portcullis, an 'outer' gate and a 'new bridge' at White Castle, and this date would not be inconsistent with the architectural details of the gatehouse into the outer ward.

Beyond is a passageway, which was closed at each end by a pair of gates and vaulted in stone with a floor above (see reconstruction, below). Within the gate-passage, there was a vaulted guard chamber to the left, with a fireplace and chimney in one wall. The

A reconstruction drawing of the outer gatehouse as it may have looked soon after 1257 (Illustration by Chris Jones-Jenkins, 1991).

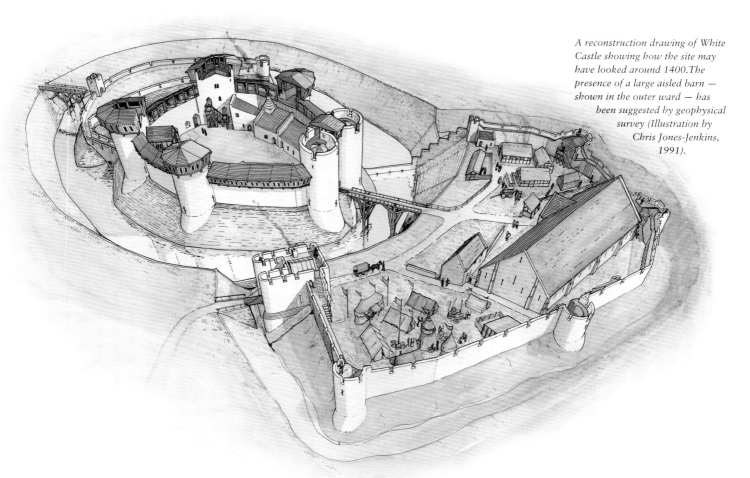

A reconstruction drawing of White Castle showing how the site may have looked around 1400. The presence of a large aisled barn — shown in the outer ward — has been suggested by geophysical survey (Illustration by Chris Jones-Jenkins, 1991).

inner wall of the guard chamber — towards the passage — was of timber, as can be seen from the straight edges of the adjacent masonry. On the opposite side of the passage is a short flight of stairs, which led to a mural passage, and to a latrine located over the ditch. The doorway to the passage has pyramidal chamfer stops at the base, of mid- or late thirteenth-century type.

Passing through the outer gatehouse, and standing in the outer ward, look at the surrounding curtain wall and towers. You will see the backs of four projecting towers, three circular and one rectangular. Each is two storeys high and each had a battlemented wall-walk. The three circular towers are virtually identical with an unlit ground-floor room and an upper floor supported on timber beams with arrowloops in embrasures, which covered both the curtain wall to each side and the ground in front. The inner walls were probably timber framed, and each would have had an external wooden stair giving access to the upper floor.

The rectangular tower was also timber backed, but it was designed on a more individual basis. Its upper room formed a small lodging, with a fireplace and its own latrine (with a deep pit discharging into the outer ditch). This room would have been the residence of a household official, perhaps a steward or quartermaster responsible for troops and supplies housed in the outer ward.

Geophysical survey has shown that the foundations of a very large rectangular building, measuring some 115 by 66 feet (35 by 20m), survive under the turf along this north-western side of the ward. It was probably an aisled barn, where the produce of the large manorial estate — of which White Castle was the centre — was processed and stored. There are traces of further buildings, probably timber framed, at the western end of the ward, near the moat. There was also a latrine here, set in a recess in the curtain wall. The slots for the wooden seat can be seen, as can the traces of its inner wall.

The rectangular tower on the curtain wall of the outer ward. The upper room may have served as the residence of the steward or quartermaster.

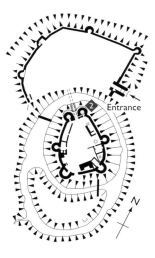

The Inner Gatehouse

The inner ward is surrounded by an impressive water-filled moat, cut deep into the red sandstone and marl, and faced with a sloping masonry revetment. A modern timber bridge, on the line of the medieval original, spans the moat. The water in the moat is controlled by two low dams of medieval stonework. The medieval bridge was only half the length of the present one, under whose inner half is

a drawbridge pit. During the Middle Ages, the bridge would have extended only as far as the outer edge of the pit, which in turn was spanned by a liftable drawbridge. When down, this drawbridge would have rested on the outer edge of the pit. When raised, the pit and the vertical decking of the bridge

A reconstruction drawing of the inner gatehouse. With the drawbridge raised, the gateway was protected by a deep pit. The portcullis, a substantial iron-shod grille, could be dropped to protect the door (Illustration by Chris Jones-Jenkins, 1991).

would have barred the way to the gatehouse (see reconstruction, opposite).

Two large circular towers flank the gate-passage. The east tower (on the left) is partly rebuilt. At some unknown date, its whole outer face collapsed into the moat, or had to be taken down and rebuilt. The small rectangular sockets in its wall face are 'putlog holes' for the beams of the timber scaffolding. A possible context for this rebuilding is provided by the record that in 1437–38 twenty-one oak trees were felled to make three new floors in each of the two gatehouse towers, but the evidence is far from conclusive.

The gatehouse itself was added to the earlier curtain wall during the mid- to later thirteenth-century rebuilding. The gate-passage has a pointed barrel vault above, and was fitted with pairs of gates at either end. The drawbar holes in which a stout timber post was placed to secure these gates can still be traced. There was a portcullis at the front of the gatehouse, the grooves for which can be seen above the entrance arch.

Each tower of the gatehouse was of four storeys, and each was entered from doorways on the inner ward side. The eastern tower (on the left-hand side as you enter) was also reached through a passageway from the gate-passage. The original doorway into this same tower from the interior of the ward is now a ruined gap. Inside, however, the steps down into the tower from the doorway still survive. There are also traces of a spiral stair that led to the upper floors. Heavy, rift-like, straight joints mark the junctions of the old work and the new. The rear face of the original tower remains, with enough detail to show that its internal arrangements were the same as those of its counterpart. In the rebuilt front part of the tower there are fireplaces on the upper two floors.

The west tower (right of the gate-passage) is entered from the ward by way of a flight of steps and a doorway, the original stonework of which has been renewed. As in the east tower, there is a spiral stair in the thickness of the inner wall, giving access to the upper floors. Here, however, the internal arrangements are much clearer. The ground floor has three arrowloops (two of which are

The defences of the inner ward were created in two phases. The curtain walls, along with the now-demolished keep, were raised in the twelfth century. The twin-towered gatehouse (to the left) and the other mural towers were added decades later, in the latter half of the thirteenth century.

The top of the inner ward gatehouse provides a good view of features of the inner ward. To the left are the foundations of two periods of hall [1]. Beyond, there is the castle well [2], what was probably the constable's accommodation [3], and the site of the chapel [4]. The small tower was levelled and its massive foundations [5] are now crossed by a stretch of curtain wall [6].

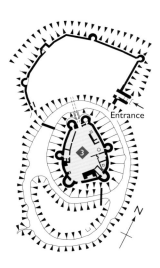

blocked in part). The stair up is arranged in short separate flights, so as to give greater protection against attackers forcing their way up the stairs.

The first floor has a single arrowloop facing west. From this point the medieval stair bypassed the second floor and carried on directly up to the third. The second floor itself is blank without openings and not only gave added height to the gatehouse and increased its command of the ground to the front, but also provided a secure storage space. The upper floor of the tower rose above the level of the curtain, and would have provided access to a small chamber between the towers at this level from which the portcullis on the front gate would have been operated. The upper floors of the gatehouse were designed for the use of the castle's constable or steward, who controlled access to the castle through the gatehouse arrangements. The dark chambers in both towers, which could only have been reached by ladder from the floors above, could have served as strongrooms for important records and valuables. Visitors who climb to the top of the stair in the north-west tower will be rewarded with a fine prospect of the landscape of north Monmouthshire and of the hills to the west. From here it is not difficult to appreciate the strategic position of White Castle amid the surrounding countryside.

The Inner Ward

The platform above the gatehouse also gives a fine bird's-eye view of the inner ward. To begin with, entry to this was from the south, at the opposite end of the ward to the main gatehouse. Two wooden bridges would have spanned the moat across the crescent-shaped island or hornwork in the distance, leading to a now-vanished archway beside a square Norman tower.

The tall curtain walls also belong to this twelfth-century phase, though they would have been simple stone walls, without the projecting defensive towers. The walls are laid out in short, straight lengths rather than in a continuous curve, a form of construction typical of the twelfth century. These first stone defences were probably the work of Ralph of Grosmont in 1184–86 (p. 5). The square Norman tower was probably still standing in 1256–57, when repairs were being made to its roof, but it was demolished soon after this, and a new section of curtain wall — with a battery of arrowloops — was built across its site. Part of the broad foundations of the tower can still be seen at the southern (far) end of the ward.

Towers and Domestic Buildings

One distinctive feature of the thirteenth-century rebuilding at White Castle, seen throughout the castle, and especially here in the inner ward, is the unusual form of arrowloop used. Cross-shaped arrowloops had come into use in the early thirteenth century, perhaps for use with crossbows. The horizontal sighting slit made it possible to line up a target before it came into the sights of an archer firing through the vertical loop. Here at White Castle, the arms of the cross loops are offset, one higher than the other. Probably the steep slopes outside the moat made it seem a good idea to have an attacker in the sights for as long a distance as possible, but like many good ideas, this one did not continue to find favour.

Inside the ward, the inner face of the curtain wall was lined with the domestic buildings of the castle. In contrast to the fine domestic apartments at Skenfrith or Grosmont, these were lightly built timber-framed structures, resting on stone sleeper walls.

Against the north-east curtain, to your left facing into the ward from the gate-passage, are the insubstantial foundations of two successive periods of hall, and the pitched-stone base of a square hearth. Beyond is the castle well and the east-central tower, one of four spaced around the external perimeter of the curtain wall. The tower was entered via a doorway cut through the older curtain, and raised about 3 feet (0.9m) above the internal ground level. The basement is unlit and must have been reached through a trapdoor in the floor of the room above. The ground-floor room has three cross-shaped arrowloops covering the curtain wall to each side, together with the ground in front. The two floors above had no openings.

Adjacent to the tower, you will see the remains of a suite of rooms probably occupied by the constable of the castle, or a similar official. The square chamber, with its fireplace of edge-set stones cut into the twelfth-century curtain, was probably a solar or sitting room. The architectural details of the fireplace, including a pair of pyramidal stops at the base, suggest that it belongs to the period when the castle was remodelled in about 1250–60. This room was originally longer, but a second room, with a fireplace of reused stones was later inserted in its outer half. A smaller room tucked into the 'corner' angle contains a large masonry latrine pit. The size of this latrine suggests that it was for the use of the garrison, rather than for the private use of occupants of this suite of rooms.

White Castle was equipped with distinctive cross-shaped arrowloops, like these in the west tower of the inner ward gatehouse. Modern research has shown that these afforded the defenders extensive coverage of the ground outside the castle.

Left: In this manuscript illustration from the early fourteenth-century Luttrell Psalter *a crossbowman prepares his bow for action (British Library, Additional Ms. 42130, f. 56).*

A thirteenth-century bone flute recovered from the moat at White Castle (National Museum of Wales).

Above: The chancel of the castle chapel was located at first-floor level in the Chapel Tower, with a timber-framed nave projecting into the courtyard.

Right: The piscina in the Chapel Tower, where the sacred vessels were washed after Mass.

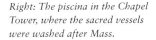

A fragment of medieval wall plaster painted to resemble fine jointed masonry in the right-hand arrowloop of the Chapel Tower.

The Chapel Tower

The second of the four mural towers is situated in the eastern angle of the curtain wall. This four-storey tower housed the castle chapel on its first floor. In 1437–38, when the gatehouse was being refloored (p. 41), 'the Great Tower called the Chapel Tower' was given a new roof and floor.

The chancel — with its altar — was located in the body of the tower itself, and was lit by three arrowloops. To the right of the central arrowloop, there is a small projecting piscina, where the sacred vessels used in the Mass were washed, and this would seem to confirm the location of the chapel at this level. The doorway at the back of the tower formed the chancel arch. The nave was situated in a timber-framed rectangular projection built against the rear of the tower. The foundations of its stone sleeper wall can be seen, with traces of the wall of an earlier building to one side of it.

In the right-hand arrowloop within the tower, remains of the original wall finish survive. The wall surfaces inside medieval rooms were generally coated in smooth white plaster, and normally painted. The most common treatment was a box pattern of fine red lines representing the mortar joints of a wall of expensive dressed freestone, as here. Similar areas of plaster survive in sheltered corners of the ruins of many medieval buildings, for example, at Tintern Abbey and Chepstow Castle. Often, as can still be seen at White Castle, the exteriors of medieval buildings were also rendered and would have been gleaming white. The present fashion for exposed stonework in medieval buildings is entirely a modern one.

The Norman Tower and Hornwork

Next to the Chapel Tower are the massive foundations of a sturdy but compact square Norman tower. This was demolished when the present south curtain wall between the towers was built over it about 1260. Its foundations were rediscovered by excavation in the 1920s. The tower is the earliest stone building known on the site, but only half remains: one complete side, and two half-sides cut off by the curtain wall. Traces of a battered base, together with a central pilaster buttress on the west survive.

The thirteenth-century curtain wall built over the demolished tower has a pair of arrowloops, and there is now a postern gate in roughly the position of the original twelfth-century entrance to the castle. Before the building of the present inner gatehouse

and the outer ward, about 1255–60, entry would have been by way of the crescent-shaped hornwork.

The hornwork itself was defended with a timber palisade and towers, and can be seen from the ground outside the postern gate. The stone wall (to the left) crossing the moat to the island is one of a pair of later medieval dams controlling the level of the water. The hornwork retains traces of stone defences, including a gateway on the east, and there was probably a round tower at the western tip (see reconstruction, p. 39).

The Kitchen, Malthouse and Bakehouse
Returning through the postern gate, the rounded tower to the visitor's left — reached down a shallow flight of steps — is perhaps the best and most accessible of the thirteenth-century towers added to the earlier Norman curtain wall. In common with the Chapel Tower described above, it has a D-shaped plan, and both are rather larger than the other towers on the gatehouse and those on the sides of the inner ward.

Here, as in the Chapel Tower, there were four stages. The lowest level had three arrowloops

covering the ground in front, and the first floor has a pair of loops covering the curtain to each side. The curious offset arms of the cross-shaped loops, so characteristic of White Castle, can be seen. The upper floors of the tower have no spiral stair and were reached by a wooden stair on the back of the tower. The third stage is blank, with no loops, and that above has been largely destroyed.

Between this tower and the gatehouse are the foundations of a range of buildings built against the inner face of the curtain wall. At the southern end, near the entry to the fourth wall tower, is a combined malthouse and bakehouse, with a rectangular malting kiln and a circular bread oven side by side. Malt was made in the kiln by roasting barley that had been allowed to germinate. After being ground, the malt and other ingredients would have been boiled in a large container, perhaps on an open hearth on the floor, to make beer. Beer was the normal drink in medieval times, when the drinking of water was considered to be a religious penance. The long narrow building beyond was probably the kitchen, where there would have been other ovens for the preparation of food.

The postern — seen here to the right of the D-shaped tower at the south-west angle of the curtain — is close to the original entrance to the twelfth-century castle. A wooden bridge from the hornwork would have approached the earlier entrance arch.

Within the castle was a combined malthouse and bakehouse, with a rectangular malting kiln and a circular oven for baking bread.

Hen Gwrt Medieval Moated Site

Unlike Skenfrith and Grosmont, White Castle does not lie next to its parish church. At the other two castles, church and village grew up outside the defences in Anglo-Norman times. White Castle is in open country, with the village of Llantilio Crossenny and its church located a mile and a half (2.4km) away to the south-east. Llantilio (Llantelyo or Llandeilo Gresynni in medieval times) means the church of St Teilo, the Welsh saint whose principal monastery was at Llandeilo Fawr in Carmarthenshire. Early charters suggest that in origin the church is much older than the castle and may have formed the centre of a large ecclesiastical estate which in medieval times belonged to the bishop of Llandaff. Throughout the Middle Ages, Llantilio Crossenny was divided between the king (Llantelyo regis, with the castle) and the bishop (Llantelyo episcopi). The bishop's manor was administered from a moated site known as Hen Gwrt (the Old Court) some 300 yards (274m) from the church.

Hen Gwrt is an excellent example of a type of monument that is not particularly common in Wales. It consists of a square grassy island surrounded by a water-filled moat. There is now no trace of the buildings that once stood upon the central island.

The medieval manor of the bishops of Llandaff later came into the ownership of the Herberts of Raglan Castle, who established a deer park — a securely ditched and fenced area a square mile (259ha) or more in extent — where red and fallow deer were kept for hunting. Hen Gwrt became a hunting lodge. Local tradition associates it with Dafydd Gam, a kinsman of the Herberts, who was killed at Agincourt (1415) and so earned a mention in Shakespeare's *Henry V*. His children are said to have been so many that with arms outstretched they could reach from Llantilio church to Hen Gwrt. Sadly, there seems to be as little basis for his association with the site as there is for the number of his progeny.

The Nature of the Buildings

In 1775 a local landowner, John Lewis, built the now demolished Llantilio Court north of the church. In 1820 the present road was diverted around the grounds of the house and it was probably then that Hen Gwrt was robbed for road metalling. The then 'Mr Lewis of Llantilio' had a plan made of 'the foundations of the Old Court, taken as they

Wooden kissing gate from road to grassed surface and wooden bridge over moat. Uneven grassed surface on island.

Stag hunting — a favourite noble pastime — in a fifteenth-century manuscript illustration. After acquiring the medieval manor of Llantelyo episcopi, the Herberts of Raglan Castle established a deer park there and Hen Gwrt became a hunting lodge (Bibliothèque Nationale, Paris Ms. Lat. 1156B, f. 163/ Bridgeman Art Library).

Opposite: Today, Hen Gwrt is little more than a grassy island surrounded by a water-filled moat: no visible traces of the medieval buildings survive.

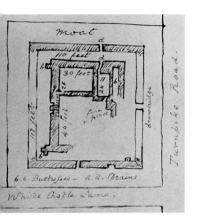

Above: 'The foundations of the Old Court, taken as they were discovered': the walls were found during stone robbing, probably for the metalling of the nearby road in 1820 (Cambrian Archaeological Association).

An aerial view of Hen Gwrt from the south (Royal Commission on the Ancient and Historical Monuments of Wales).

were discovered'. By the time the moat came into the guardianship of the predecessors of Cadw in 1941, it was covered in trees. Excavation and clearance of the site showed that very little of the buildings planned by Lewis had survived the stone robbing. Some traces were found of a timber building associated with thirteenth/fourteenth-century pottery and belonging to the bishop's manor.

Lewis's plan shows a squarish stone building in the centre of the moated area, with a substantial stone wall around the edge of the ditch. This can be identified as the fifteenth- to sixteenth-century

hunting lodge of the Herberts. A wooden bridge (one of the main beams of which survives in situ) crossed the moat. Within the central building, Lewis's plan shows a large room with fireplace, possibly a hall, with a smaller chamber, to the north. A pair of small rooms with drains to one side of this may be a latrine. A pair of recesses in the west wall may mark the position of two latrine chutes from the upper floor. The deer park, and probably the hunting lodge, were destroyed when Raglan Castle was taken from the royalist Herberts by parliament at the end of the Civil War (1642–48).

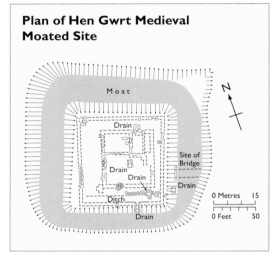

Plan of Hen Gwrt Medieval Moated Site

Further Reading

J. A. Bradney, *A History of Monmouthshire, volume I, part I, Hundred of Skenfrith* (1904); facsimile edition (London 1991).

D. A. Carpenter, *The Minority of Henry III* (London 1990).

O. E. Craster and J. M. Lewis, 'Hen Gwrt Moated Site', *Archaeologia Cambrensis* 112 (1963), 159–183.

O. E. Craster, 'Skenfrith Castle: When was it built?', *Archaeologia Cambrensis* 116 (1967), 133–158.

O. E. Craster, *Skenfrith Castle* (HMSO, London 1970).

David Crouch, *William Marshal: Knighthood, War and Chivalry 1147–1219*, second edition (London 2002).

R. R. Davies, *Lordship and Society in the March of Wales 1282–1400* (Oxford 1978).

R. R. Davies, *Conquest, Coexistence and Change: Wales 1063–1415* (Oxford 1987); reprinted in paperback as, *The Age of Conquest: Wales 1063–1415* (Oxford 1991).

Ralph Griffiths, Tony Hopkins and Ray Howell (eds), *The Gwent County History, Volume 2: The Age of the Marcher Lords, c. 1070–1536* (Cardiff 2008).

C. Ellis, *Hubert de Burgh, A Study in Constancy* (London 1952).

Jeremy K. Knight, *Grosmont Castle* (HMSO, Cardiff 1980).

Jeremy K. Knight, 'The Road to Harlech: Aspects of Some Early Thirteenth-Century Welsh Castles', in J. R. Kenyon and R. Avent (eds), *Castles in Wales and the Marches* (Cardiff 1987), 75–88.

John Newman, *The Buildings of Wales: Gwent/Monmouthshire* (Harmondsworth 2000)

A. J. Roderick and W. Rees, 'The Lordships of Abergavenny, Grosmont, Skenfrith and White Castle: Accounts of the Ministers for the year 1256–57', *South Wales and Monmouth Record Society Publications* 2 (1953), 68–125; 3 (1954), 22–47.

C. A. R. Radford, *White Castle* (HMSO, London 1962).